Special Effects in Film

Simon Page and Mark Warner

Series Editors: Steve Barlow and Steve Skidmore

Published by Ginn and Company
Halley Court, Jordan Hill, Oxford OX2 8EJ
A division of Reed Educational and Professional Publishing Ltd

OXFORD MELBOURNE AUCKLAND JOHANNESBURG BLANTYRE
GABORONE IBADAN PORTSMOUTH (NH) USA CHICAGO

Telephone number for ordering **Impact**: 01865 888084

© Simon Page and Mark Warner 1999

First published 1999

2003 2002 2001 2000 99

10 9 8 7 6 5 4 3 2 1

ISBN 0 435 21264 8

Illustrations
Keith Page

Picture Research
Mags Robertson

Cover photograph
Moviestore Collection

Designed by Shireen Nathoo Design

Printed and bound in Spain by Eldelvives

Acknowledgements
The Authors and Publishers wish to thank the following for permission to reproduce
photographs on the pages noted:
Aquarius Library pp. 14, 44; Corbis/Everett p.20; Kobal Collection
pp. 5, 9, 13, 15, 16, 17, 24, 30, 31, 32, 40, 41, 43, 45; Moviestore/Aardman
pp. 28–9; Moviestore Collection pp. 4, 5, 6, 7, 8, 18, 19, 21, 30, 33, 36–7, 38–9,
40, 42, 47; The Ronald Grant Archive pp. 10–11, 27, 34–5, 39.

Tel: 01865 888058 email: info.he@heinemann.co.uk

Contents

Introduction

Film-makers use special effects (SFX) to amaze and entertain people.

But what are SFX and how do they work? This book shows how the impossible is made to happen before our very eyes.

The *Titanic* sank in 1912. However, it sailed again in the blockbusting film, *Titanic*.

▲ *The* Titanic *about to sink again!*

Dinosaurs do not wander the Earth any more. But Steven Spielberg brought them back to life in *Jurassic Park*.

Jurassic Park *dinosaurs.* ►

▲ Independence Day *and the White House explodes!*

The White House in America is still standing, even though aliens blew it to pieces in *Independence Day*.

These scenes could only happen using the magic of SFX.

Stunts

DANGER!

Very few actors do their own stunts. Too many risks are involved. When you see a hero jump from an aeroplane or crash a car, you are often watching a stuntperson at work.

DID YOU KNOW?

Circus acrobats and cowboys used to do stunts in early films. They had great skill but they were not paid well. The best stuntpeople today can earn around £100,000 for one stunt.

▲ *A stuntperson at work in* A License to Kill.

Some stunts need a stuntperson to be set on fire.

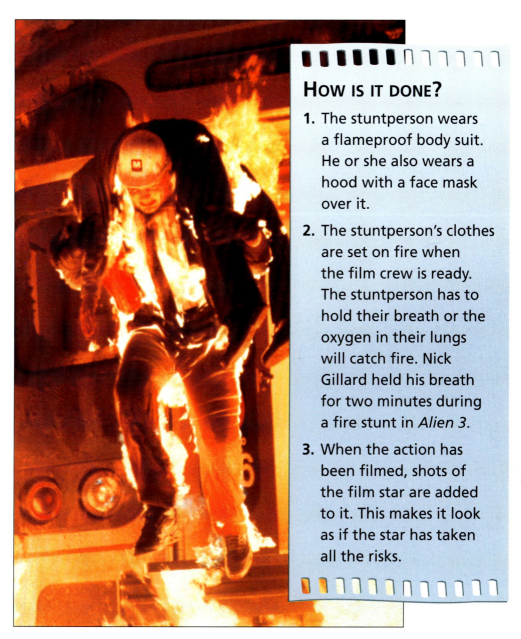

How is it done?

1. The stuntperson wears a flameproof body suit. He or she also wears a hood with a face mask over it.

2. The stuntperson's clothes are set on fire when the film crew is ready. The stuntperson has to hold their breath or the oxygen in their lungs will catch fire. Nick Gillard held his breath for two minutes during a fire stunt in *Alien 3*.

3. When the action has been filmed, shots of the film star are added to it. This makes it look as if the star has taken all the risks.

▲ *A stuntperson feels the heat in* Volcano.

PROPS

Action films often show someone crashing through
a window.

The SFX team makes special props for the stuntperson to
jump through. The stuntperson wears padded clothing and
falls onto thick mattresses.

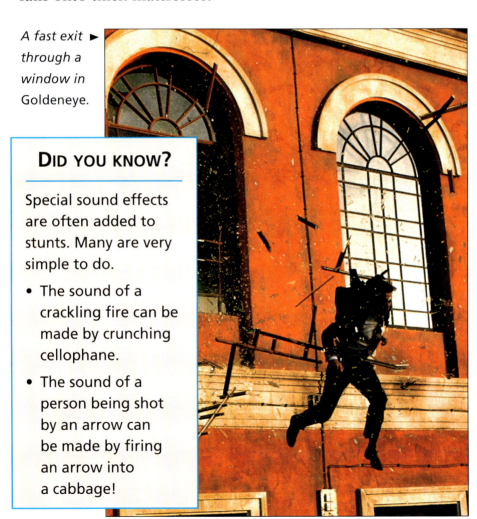

*A fast exit ▶
through a
window in*
Goldeneye.

Some stunts look dangerous but are safe. An actor in *The Godfather* played the part of a man called Sonny who was killed by gunmen. The SFX team made the shooting look real.

HOW WAS IT DONE?

1. The actor's clothes were covered in small explosive charges.

2. The actor was 'shot' – small pellets of fake blood were fired at him.

3. The explosive charges were set off at the same time. It made the shooting look real.

▲ *Sonny was shot in* The Godfather. *The stunt was so safe that a stuntperson was not needed.*

Making the weather

SNOW

Snowfalls, strong winds and rainstorms are often needed
in a film.

Sometimes an SFX team has to create them. They use
a studio or the place where the film is being shot. Filming
a real snowstorm can be costly and dangerous. Snow scenes
are usually shot in a studio where the SFX team can be
in control.

Creating a snowstorm on a hot day in Hollywood is quite normal in the film world!

▼ *Bruce Willis in* Die Hard II. *Over 45,000kg of fake snow was used to create a huge snowstorm.*

WIND

Wind machines are used to make strong winds. The largest wind machines work with the help of aircraft engines.

In *Twister*, a tornado blew across America. People, cars and even houses were swept up and tossed aside. Even the biggest wind machines could not make the strong winds needed in *Twister*.

The SFX team created some of the action.

DID YOU KNOW?

Fog can be created by feeding dry ice into a wind machine.

How was it done?

1. Stunt people were filmed being blown about.

2. These pictures were mixed with shots of a real tornado.

3. **Computer generated images (CGI)** of lightning and wild weather were added.

▲ *Strong winds about to hit parts of America in* Twister.

All change!

CHANGING A FACE

SFX make-up artists can change an actor's face. They can turn someone into a monster or make them look injured. It often takes a long time to put this make-up on.

▼ *Two of the roles played by Eddie Murphy in* The Nutty Professor. *He played all five members of a family. The SFX make-up artist made each one looked different.*

One of Batman's enemies fell into a huge tub of acid in *Batman*. A terrible fixed smile was burned onto his face. He hid his face with make-up that made him look like a clown. He called himself 'The Joker'.

▼ *Make-up and wire gave The Joker a fixed smile in* Batman.

HOW WAS IT DONE?

1. The SFX team used small wires to pull apart each side of the actor's mouth. This made a fixed smile.

2. Clown make-up was then painted on. The Joker was born.

CHANGING A BODY

Sometimes an actor plays the part of a monster or alien. The SFX team often need to give the actor full body make-up.

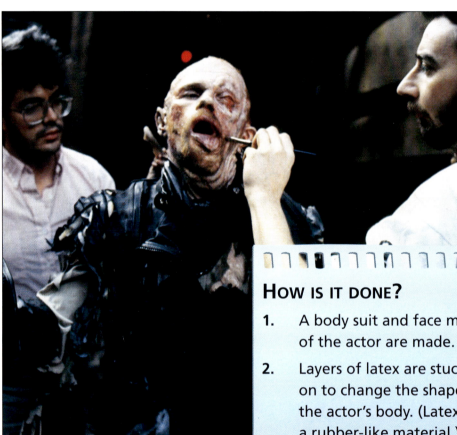

▲ *An actor being made up in* Robocop.

🔲🔲🔲🔲🔲🔲🔲🔲🔲🔲🔲🔲🔲🔲

HOW IS IT DONE?

1. A body suit and face mask of the actor are made.

2. Layers of latex are stuck on to change the shape of the actor's body. (Latex is a rubber-like material.)

3. The body suit and face mask are painted.

4. A costume is added to make it look even more terrible.

🔲🔲🔲🔲🔲🔲🔲🔲🔲🔲🔲🔲🔲🔲

▼ *The final effect in* Robocop.

Morphing

CHANGED ON COMPUTER

Morphing is a special effect created by mixing computer images with live action. This means that an actor can change size or shape without make-up or body suits. Even an actor's face can be changed!

▼ *Morphing was used to change the shape of Jim Carrey's face in* The Mask.

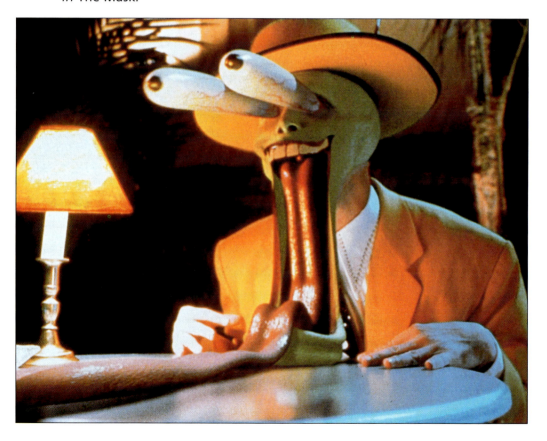

In *Death Becomes Her*, an actor was changed by morphing.

▲ *Morphing was used to turn Meryl Streep's head round in* Death Becomes Her.

HOW WAS IT DONE?

1. The actor wore a hood to hide her head. Then she was filmed.

2. The actor hid her body. Then she was filmed again.

3. The two shots of the actor's head and body were fed into a computer. Then they were 'morphed' together.

4. The final shot made it look as if her head was turned back to front!

THE BEST!

James Cameron is a film director who uses amazing special effects. In *The Abyss*, he mixed computer graphics with live action to make a 3D snake from water. The snake changed its shape to reflect the face of anyone who looked at it.

▲ *James Cameron's SFX in* The Abyss.

In *Terminator 2 – Judgement Day*, James Cameron made a metal robot walk out of a fire. He then morphed it back into the shape of a human being.

▲ *James Cameron's SFX in* Terminator 2 – Judgement Day. *The film won an Oscar for Best Visual Effects.*

Trick shots

The first 'moving pictures' were shown around one hundred years ago. People were amazed that real life could be shown on a screen.

But people wanted more than moving pictures of real life. They wanted stories.

Film-makers needed to make the stories seem real. They used sets, props, actors, costumes and make-up. Before long they used tricks as well. These were the first special effects.

▲ The Man with the Rubber Head *was made in 1901 by a Frenchman called George Melies. It included some of the first trick shots in film.*

To make the SFX for *The Man with the Rubber Head*, George Melies 'pumped up' his own head.

HOW WAS IT DONE?

1. George Melies filmed the background shot. The space above the table was left black.

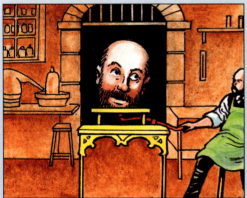

2. He then put the same strip of film through the camera again. This time he filmed his head. He made sure it would appear in the black space above the table.

3. He made his head appear bigger by moving towards the camera as it filmed him.

Compositing

Compositing means mixing pictures together. This is an important special effect. It can make impossible things seem real.

DID YOU KNOW?

There are many ways of mixing pictures together. Another way is to paint a picture onto glass. This is then mixed with another shot. This is known as **matte painting**.

▲ *Christopher Reeve as Superman seems to fly above the city of Metropolis.*

The shot of Superman flying above Metropolis was made possible by using **front projection.**

HOW WAS IT DONE?

1. In front projection, the camera films through a two-way mirror.

2. The background of Metropolis was projected onto the screen.

3. This was mixed with the actor's image.

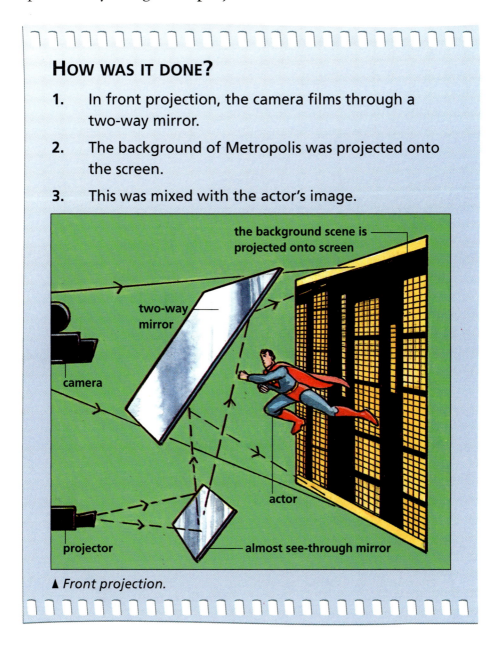

▲ *Front projection.*

Animation

ANIMATION USING DRAWINGS

Animation films such as cartoons make 'moving pictures' from still images.

A cartoon can be made by drawing in the corner of several pieces of paper. Each picture shows a small change from the one before. The pictures tell a story. Flicking through the pages brings the story to life. In other words it 'animates' the story.

Films such as *Anastasia* use this kind of trick. Teams of animators work on the film.

▲ Anastasia *was made up from about 65,000 pictures.*

ANIMATION USING MODELS

Models can also be used to make animation films. They are often made from wood or clay. This way of making films takes a lot of time.

HOW IS IT DONE?

1. The models are filmed one or two frames at a time.

2. Between each frame the models are moved slightly.

3. They are then filmed again.

4. When all the frames are put together, the models appear to move.

Wallace and Gromit about to ► *become heroes in* The Wrong Trousers. *The British animator, Nick Park, used models. He won an Oscar for this film.*

ANIMATION AND LIVE ACTION

Mixing animation with live action is another special effect. This can be difficult for the actors. They have to pretend the cartoon characters are acting with them in a scene.

▲ *Disney's* Mary Poppins *mixed live action with cartoons. The cartoons were drawn on clear sheets known as cells.*

Who Framed Roger Rabbit? ▶ *was set in Toon Town. It starred British actor, Bob Hoskins.*

COMPUTER ANIMATION

Tron was the first film to mix live action with computer animation. It was a big step forward in special effects. But Disney lost money on the film.

After that, computer graphics were not used in film for a few years. Then *Terminator 2* showed what was possible with computer graphics.

Disney made *Toy Story* in 1996. It was the first full-length film to be animated using computers.

◄ *Over 100 computers were needed to make the adventures of Buzz Lightyear and Woody in* Toy Story.

Making monsters and creatures

SFX teams must make monsters and creatures look real. They must also make them move as if they are real. The background needs to fit in with the monsters and creatures. People watching the film must feel that they are seeing real-life action.

Willis O'Brien was the first master of movie monsters. He used **stop-motion animation** to film *King Kong* in 1933.

▲ *The stop-motion animation in* King Kong *was very slow. It took over a year to make the film.*

SFX monsters and creatures can now be created on computers as they were in *Godzilla* and *Jurassic Park*.

This means that a monster or creature can be made to look blurred when it moves quickly. It mixes with the live action in a way that looks real.

But large models are also used. These are built by teams of sculptors and model-makers.

◄ *A dinosaur from* Jurassic Park.

DID YOU KNOW?

Large creatures or monsters can be made by covering steel frames with foam **latex** skin. These are then used for close shots. Other shots may involve actors wearing creature suits.

Sets

MAKING SETS

Film-makers have built sets since movies began. These are places where the action in the film takes place. Some sets are made using models.

Sets are used instead of real buildings because the film-maker has control of them. It is also not against the law to blow them up!

This set for You Only Live Twice ▶ *was built in England.*

BLOWING SETS UP

Film-makers often blow up a set or model after it has
been built!

Experts use many types of bombs so that each explosion
looks different. The explosions are set off by electronic fuses.
The action is filmed by high speed cameras. Shots are needed
from many different angles.

Model buildings were blown up in *Independence Day*. The models were 'scored' before they exploded. Scoring means sections were cut away. This meant that each model had a weak place. The experts could then be sure in which direction the blast would go.

▼ *An explosion in* Independence Day. *The people were mixed with shots of the model afterwards. This made the action seem real.*

EXPLOSION!

Explosions are planned very carefully. They are dangerous
and they cost a lot to make.

The White House was built as a small model in
Independence Day. It was then filled with dolls' house
furniture.

Nine high-speed cameras filmed the explosion of The
White House. The final shot showed the model of The White
House mixed with an alien space craft. The space craft was
not a model. It was created on computer.

▲ *The White House exploding in* Independence Day.

◄ *The model of the White House before the explosion in* Independence Day.

39

Ships and space

EXPLOSIONS IN SPACE

Film-makers can use stunning SFX for films set in space. Two of the greatest film-makers in history have used SFX to tell stories about space.

◄ *Steven Spielberg made* Close Encounters of the Third Kind *and* ET The Extra-Terrestrial.

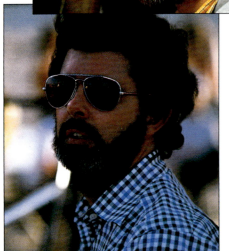

Star Wars was made in 1977. It used SFX that had never been used before. For the first time, an explosion was made to look as though it happened with no gravity. It was known as the 'zero gravity explosion'.

▲ *George Lucas made the* Star Wars *films.*

Special effects make an explosion in space.

HOW WAS IT DONE?

1. Explosives were placed on the ceiling of the set.

2. The camera was placed on the ground.

3. The explosion was set off. It blew downward so that it looked like it was happening in space or 'zero gravity'.

BLUE SCREEN

The spaceships in the *Star Wars* films were filmed in front of a **blue screen.**

The background was filmed separately. Holes the size and shape of spaceships were left in the background image.

Then the two pieces of film were printed together onto a new film. This was done using an **optical printer.**

The blue screen shots of the X-wing fighter attack.

The Imperial Snow Walkers in *The Empire Strikes Back* were filmed using blue screen shots. The SFX team used two different sizes of models.

Small models were used ▶
for long shots.

Large models were used for close up shots.

Industrial Light and Magic (ILM)

Industrial Light and Magic (ILM) is an SFX company. It was started by George Lucas, the director of *Star Wars*. George Lucas wanted to bring SFX experts together to make *Star Wars* special.

The ILM special effects team used **motion control** in *Star Wars*. Motion-controlled cameras are moved around using a computer. They can repeat the same movements as often as is needed.

The spacecraft fights in Star Wars were filmed by motion-controlled cameras. This made the shots very realistic. People watching the film felt as if they were flying the spacecraft!

ILM has made the special effects for many top films. It has also won many Oscars and awards for technical achievement.

There are now many other SFX companies. Their experts keep finding new ways to make the impossible happen. Such as how to build a new *Titanic* and sink it again!

▲ *The trick of a successful SFX is to make it look real. This shot from* Titanic *was made using computers and models. But people are made to feel they are seeing the 'real'* Titanic.

Special effects – the future!

Film was invented about one hundred years ago. What might films look like in another hundred years' time?

VIRTUAL REALITY

Films may be watched on **virtual reality headsets** instead of at the cinema. The SFX may be so real that the person watching the film will feel as if they are part of it.

HOLOGRAMS

Films might be made into **holograms** and watched in 3D.

COMPUTERS

Films could be made only on computers. New SFX may mean that real-life actors are not used any more.

- Film directors could create new actors on screen.
- Stars from the past could be recreated on screen and made to act again.

The possibilities for film are endless. One thing is certain. Special effects look more real and are getting bigger and better all the time.

Might John Wayne act again in films of the future?

Glossary

blue screen A way of mixing images together by filming in front of a blue screen. The blue screen is replaced in the film by the chosen background. *page 42*

compositing Mixing pictures together to create one film image. *page 24*

computer generated imagery (CGI) Images used in a film that have been created in a computer. *page 13*

front projection Mixing actors with a chosen background by filming them in front of a projected image. *page 25*

hologram A form of photograph which produces a 3D image. *page 46*

latex A type of rubber material used in face and body make up. *page 16, 33*

matte painting Mixing an image with a background painted onto glass. *page 24*

motion control The use of a camera which has its movements controlled by a computer instead of a person. *page 44*

optical printer A special film camera which mixes images from different film strips into a single image. *page 42*

stop-motion animation The use of pictures or models to create moving pictures. They are photographed a frame at a time and moved between each shot. *page 32*

virtual reality headset A helmet which can take the person wearing it into a world created by a computer. *page 46*

wind machine A large fan used to create windy conditions. *page 12*